FRENCH ENGLISH PICTURE DICTIONARY

 SUMMARY

- Family
- House
- Fruit and Vegetables
- Transport
- Animals

My sister
Ma soeur

my **Grandmother**
Ma grand-mère

My Grandfather
Mon grand-père

Auntie
Tante

Cousin
Cousin

Cousine
Cousine

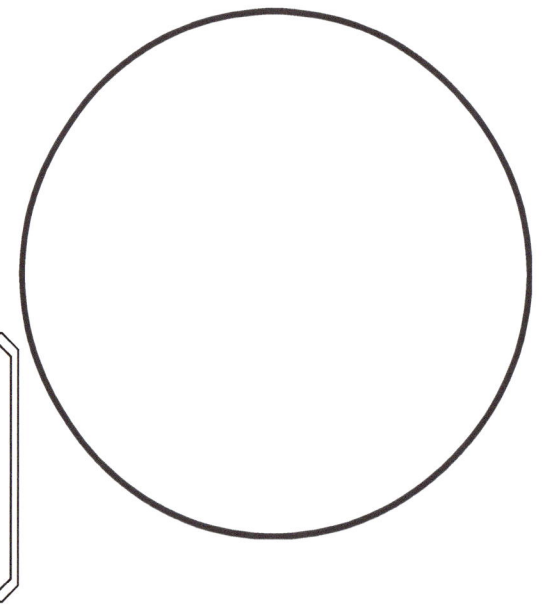

Uncle
Oncle

Cousine
Cousine

Cousin
Cousin

Boy
Fils

Daughter
Fille

Granddaughter
Petit-fille

Grandson
Petit-fils

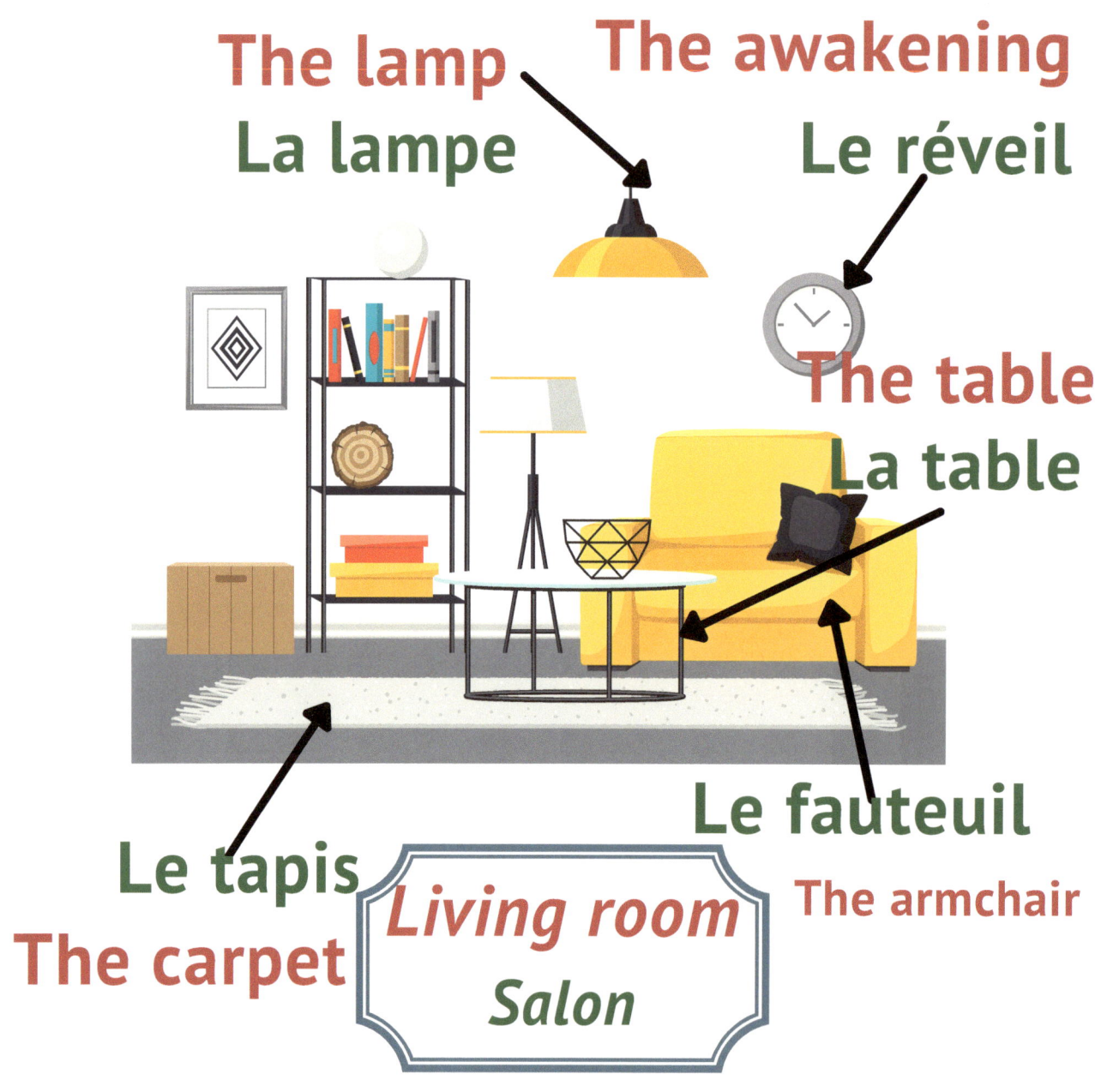

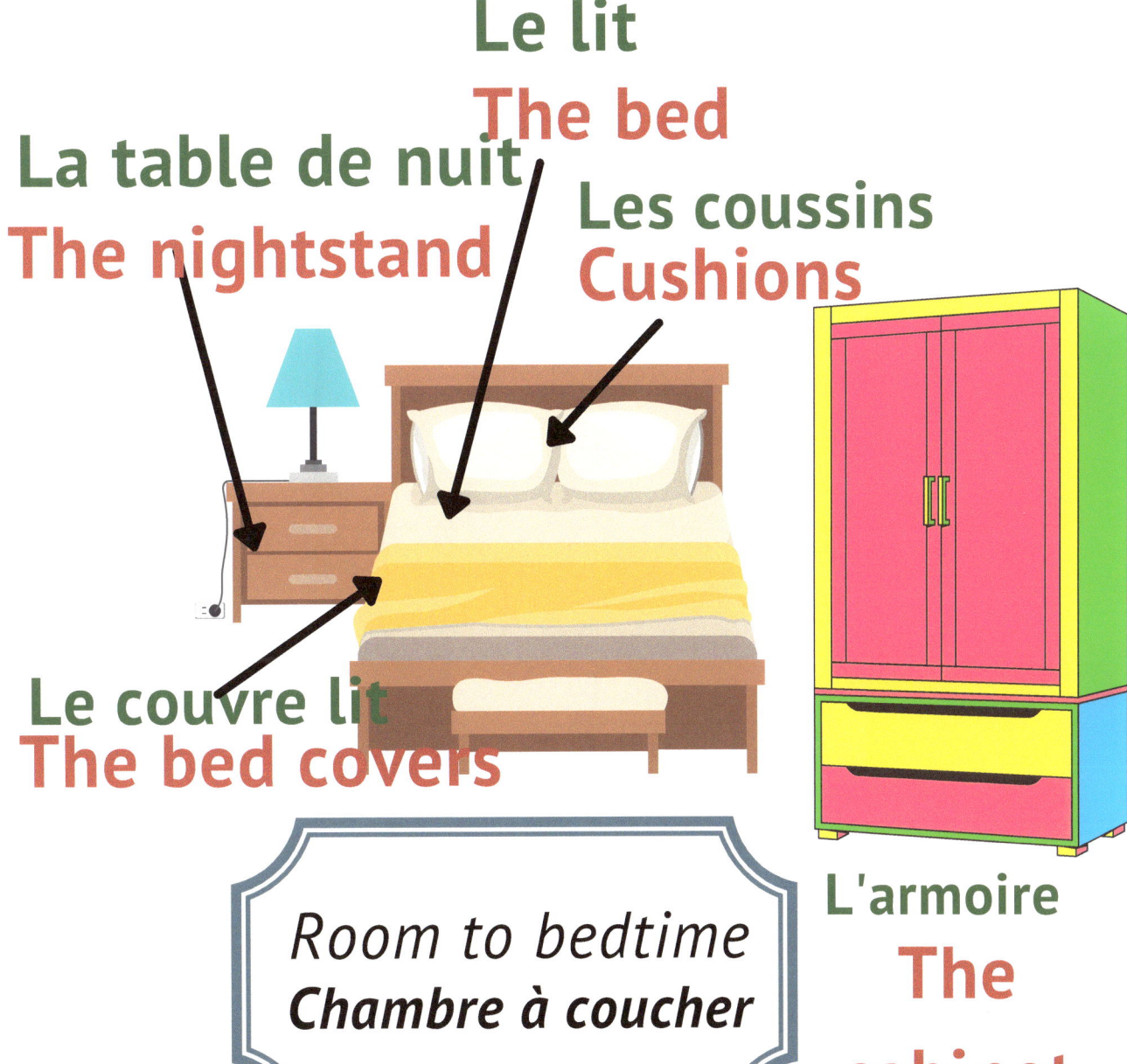

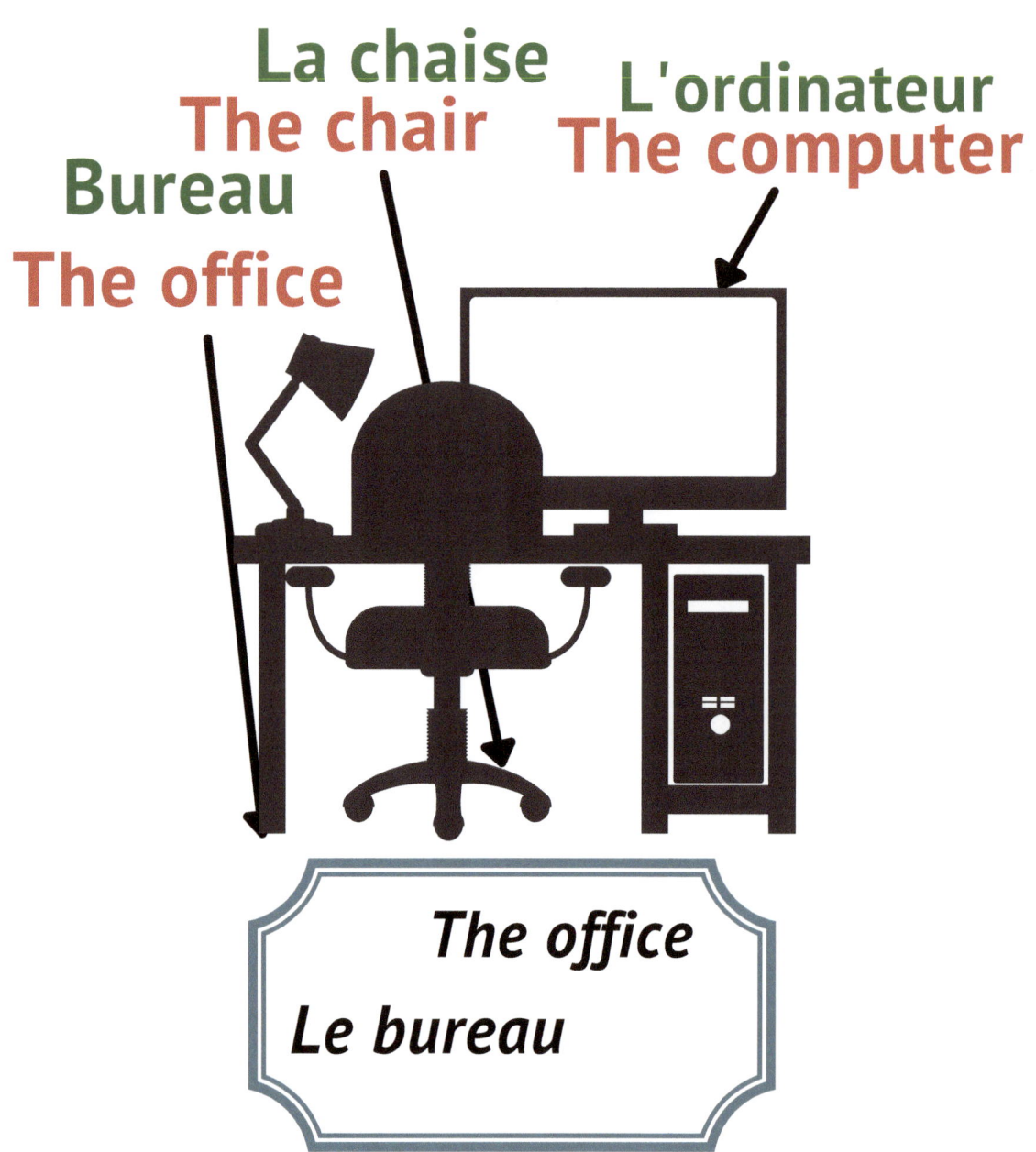

The kitchen
La cuisine

Cooking pot
La marmite

The pan
La casserole

The kettle
La bouilloire

The blender
Le mixeur

The plate
L'assiette

The spoon
La cuillère

The ladle
La louche

Fork
Fourchette

The knife
Le couteau

The whip
Le fouet

The plateau
Le plateau

The bowl
Le bol

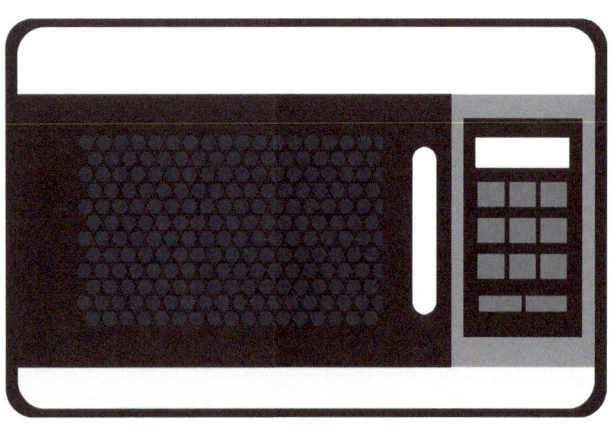

The oven
Le four

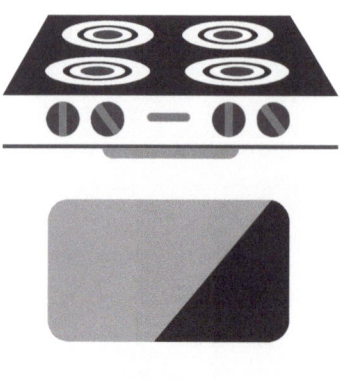

The cook
La cuisinière

The fridge
Le frigo

The washing machine
La machine à laver

Légumes
vegetables

Beans

Haricots

Brussels sprouts

Chou de Bruxelles

Artichoke

Artichaut

Broccoli

Brocoli

pepper

Poivron

Carrot

Carotte

Eggplant
Aubergine

Garlic
Ail

Tomato
Tomate

Onion
Oignon

Courgette
Courgette

potato
Patate

Lettuce
Laitue

Beet
Betterave

Radish
Radis

Cucumber
Concombre

maize
Maïs

Fruits fruit

Banana

Banane

Apricot

Abricot

Apple

Pomme

Fig
Figue

watermelon
Pastèque

Grape
Raisin

Orange
Orange

Pineapple
Ananas

Kiwi
Kiwi

Strawberry

Fraise

Grenada

Grenade

Pear

Poire

transport
transports

Bicycle

Bicyclette

Motorcycle

Moto

Car

Voiture

Subway

Métro

Airplane

Avion

Bus

Bus

truck

Camion

Boat

Bateau

Cat
Chat

Rabbit
Lapin

Rooster
Coq

Sheep
Mouton

Snake
Serpent

Pigeon
Pigeon

Tortoise
Tortue

Monkey
Singe

Lion
Lion

Elephant
Eléphant

Cow
Vache

Wolf
Loup

Goat
Chèvre

Lightning Source UK Ltd.
Milton Keynes UK
UKHW052037170522
403158UK00002B/166